There is great aliveness in these haiku. They are awake, and awakening. Mitsu Suzuki allows the subtle voice of dharma, of feeling, of the passing seasons and precious moments of a life well cared for to permeate her haiku with such tender clarity, they ring true like the sound of a mountain temple bell carrying through the mist. Thanks to her subtle poetic sensibility, insight, and skill, translator Kate McCandless has given us a treasure. These poems possess the Zen spirit and heart of an unassuming but wise poet whose true kindness is the greatest teacher of all. Read them quietly; they will enter your heart.

—Peter Levitt, author of
One Hundred Butterflies and *Within Within*

Mitsu Suzuki's haiku are tea water held in the bowl of the dharma, spilling with all the colors and fragrances of a human life. Reading these distilling and enlarging poems, I find myself companioned in ways I cannot name but feel completely.

—Jane Hirshfield, author of
Come, Thief and *The Heart of Haiku*

A White Tea Bowl

A WHITE TEA BOWL

100 Haiku from 100 Years of Life

Mitsu Suzuki

WITH AN INTRODUCTION BY
Norman Fischer

Translated by Kate McCandless
Edited by Kazuaki Tanahashi

SHAMBHALA · BOULDER · 2014

Shambhala Publications, Inc.
4720 Walnut Street
Boulder, Colorado 80301
www.shambhala.com

A Rodmell Press book

© 2014 by San Francisco Zen Center

Cover photograph © iStockphoto
Author photograph © Mitsue Nagase

Printed in the United States of America

♾ This edition is printed on acid-free paper that meets the American National Standards Institute Z39.48 Standard.
♻ Shambhala Publications makes every effort to print on recycled paper. For more information please visit www.shambhala.com.
Distributed in the United States by Penguin Random House LLC and in Canada by Random House of Canada Ltd

Translator: Kate McCandless
Project editor: Kazuaki Tanahashi
Editors: Donald Moyer, Holly Hammond
Design: Gopa & Ted2, Inc.
Production editor: Linda Cogozzo

Library of Congress Cataloging-in-Publication Data
Suzuki, Mitsu, 1914– author.
[Poems. Selections. English]
A white tea bowl: 100 haiku from 100 years of life/Mitsu Suzuki; with an introduction by Norman Fischer; translated by Kate McCandless; edited by Kazuaki Tanahashi.—First edition.
pages cm
ISBN 978-1-930485-35-8 (paperback)
1. Haiku—Translations into English. I. McCandless, Kate, translator. II. Tanahashi, Kazuaki, 1933– III. Title.
PL838.U9214A2 2014
895.6'15—dc23
2013046856

Contents

INTRODUCTION

Norman Fischer

In the summer of 2010, I went with a group of close students and friends on pilgrimage to Japan. We spent a week at Rinso-in, the original temple of Shunryu Suzuki Roshi, founder of San Francisco Zen Center and of our Zen practice lineage in America. Author of the most widely read of all Zen books, *Zen Mind, Beginner's Mind*, Suzuki Roshi was a beloved spiritual master. He was also Mitsu Suzuki's husband. Her years with him, and all that they brought to her life, certainly fed the silent depths whose waters gave rise to the exquisite poems that make up this book.

Rinso-in is a relatively small temple in Yaizu, formerly a fishing village, now a port city on the Pacific Ocean. In style and feeling, it is a far cry from the large Japanese Zen training monasteries, famous (if not legendary) for their tough practice. The students and friends I brought—many of whom were Zen priests—had all practiced Zen with me for many years in the United States. I myself have never trained in Japan and do not emphasize Japanese ways in my teaching. But I wanted my closest students to experience the feeling and flavor of the Zen that Suzuki Roshi expressed, the simple life of caring for a temple and its members that he had lived at Rinso-in, and that his son and successor, Hoitsu Suzuki, still lived.

We spent the week sitting in Rinso-in's small zendo, chanting in its Buddha Hall, cleaning around the temple, and watching Chitose, Hoitsu Roshi's wife, and their son Shungo, who is also a priest, and his wife Kumi, take care of the many tasks necessary to serve a local community of farmers and small-business people. The busy, if also essentially peaceful, life flowed all around us as we foreigners sat zazen, talked, drank tea, cooked our meals, and cleaned around the temple.

Mitsu Suzuki lives with her daughter a fifteen-minute drive from Rinso-in. We phoned to wish her well, not expecting to see her. At ninety-six (her age in 2010) she deserved by now some peace and quiet, and we had been told that she was no longer receiving visitors, especially people from her San Francisco days, because the effort to speak and listen in English was becoming too difficult. But when one of our group who had been a close tea ceremony student spoke to her on the phone, she said she wanted to come to meet us. We were surprised and delighted.

Okusan, as we had been used to calling her, arrived at the temple with a burst of energy. She bustled straight past us into the Buddha Hall, where she immediately made prostrations and said quiet, concentrated prayers, her head bowed, her prayer beads in her hand. She then got up without assistance and said loudly in English, beaming, "Welcome home!" We were touched by this, thinking she referred to us—that, as students inspired by Suzuki Roshi, his temple was in some way our real home. But later we realized she was saying this to herself—"Welcome home, Mitsu, to the place where your heart is kept."

We sat for a long while having tea and cookies. She spoke English astonishingly well, as we sat on the tatami floor, she on a little chair, to preserve her knees, she said. She was like a queen holding court, self-contained and dignified, still able to hold her trim, tiny body as she had always done, energetically upright, with elegant hand gestures accompanying her words. She had brought photo albums of Suzuki Roshi in the old days. "Here," she showed us, "is Suzuki Roshi at the moment of leaving Rinso-in for the last time," Hoitsu behind him, the two priests, father and son, enjoying a private joke long gone by now.

She had also brought a copy of *Love Haiku*, an anthology edited and translated by Patricia Donegan, in which two of her haiku appeared. Then she recited another haiku in Japanese, which had recently won a prize.

No limit
to kindness—
winter violets

After a while, when she tired of English, she went on energetically in Japanese, with one of our group translating. When asked how she kept so fit in body and mind, she replied, "I walk around the neighborhood every day for an hour. I make sure to say hello to those who live alone." She mentioned in particular the school next door for children who "can't go to school"—she visits them every day, bringing small gifts and good cheer—and the businessmen's boardinghouse on the other side, where many men come and go, staying only for a day or two.

At the end of her visit, a traditional children's song about spring bubbled up from her memory. She continued to sing as she strode out of our sight to her waiting car and driver, her crisp white *hippari* and matching white pants hardly making a sound as she glided away. Her sudden absence left the room somehow sadly empty, though the group of us filled it well enough. For years in America, teaching tea ceremony and Japanese ways was her practice. Now, apparently, it was kindness.

....

The long life of Mitsu Suzuki (she will be one hundred on April 23, 2014) is an unrepeatable marvel. Spanning the changes and disasters of one of the most spectacular centuries in history—one in which East and West have been struggling to meet and understand one another—the winds of time have blown her back and forth across the ocean. Beneath her sweetness, one senses the stoic toughness she possesses not so much because she was raised to it but because it was required of her. She was born in Shizuoka City in 1914, at the height of Japanese militarism and competition with the West. Her mother died when she was eleven, leaving Mitsu the woman of the household. At nineteen, dissatisfied with the conventionality and coldness she found in Japanese Buddhism, she converted to Christianity, becoming a member of the local Methodist Church. In 1936, at twenty-two, she married Masaharu Matsuno, a naval pilot. When war broke out in 1937 between China and Japan, Masaharu went off, with Mitsu seven months pregnant. He was killed just two weeks after seeing the first photographs of his daughter.

After the war, Mitsu trained as a schoolteacher, and when her daughter was three, began teaching at a local kindergarten. When the Pacific War began (the war Americans know as World War II) and American pilots began flying their interminable and devastating raids over Japan, Mitsu and the other teachers would take their students into bunkers every day as bombs rained down on the city. On the night of June 16, 1945, just three months before Japan surrendered, the entire city of Shizuoka was burned to the ground.

Mitsu, like almost all Japanese of her generation, had been brought up to believe—and had experienced it as a fact—that Americans wanted to kill her and her countrymen. How strange, marvelous, and probably disturbing then that by the early 1960s she would find herself living in the United States, the new wife of a Soto Zen priest stationed in San Francisco. A working Japanese Christian single mother would not have been able to imagine such a thing in 1940. Yet it happened.

After the war, the schools of Japan were in terrible shape, most of them closed, their facilities destroyed. Civic leaders everywhere rushed to take care of this problem as fast as they could. In Yaizu, Shunryu Suzuki was keen to reopen the historically important kindergarten attached to Rinso-in. He had been told of Mitsu by a mutual friend and was determined to hire her to run the school, though she insisted she would not leave Shizuoka, and that, in any case, how could a Christian woman run a Buddhist school? But Shunryu was extremely persistent. He kept reappearing in Shizuoka again and again to ask Mitsu to simply come visit the school. Finally she agreed. One visit was enough to convince her to take the job. As for the Christian problem? "Well at least you have some religion," he told her.

Shunryu visited the school daily, leading the children in chanting and Buddhist lessons. He and Mitsu became close colleagues and friends—two strong, opinionated, and charismatic people, with lively senses of humor. Then tragedy befell the Suzuki family: Shunryu's wife was killed by a mentally ill priest whom he'd allowed to stay at the temple during one of his absences. He was left with three young children. He needed a wife. The Rinso-in community (including Shunryu's mother-in-law) quickly agreed that Mitsu was the only possible choice.

The two were married in the fall of 1958. He was fifty-four, she was forty-four. Within the year, he had been invited to become abbot of Soko-ji temple in San Francisco, fulfilling his lifelong dream of going to America to teach Zen to Westerners. His short-term appointments to Soko-ji kept being renewed, and the longer he remained in America, the more young Western students began to come to practice zazen—not necessarily what the temple members were interested in. Eventually Shunryu turned over Rinso-in to Hoitsu, resigned his post at Soko-ji, and threw in his lot entirely with the young Western students. By 1961 Mitsu had come to join him. She remained for thirty-two years—returning home in 1994, twenty-three years after Shunryu's death. During those years Mitsu Suzuki became—by the account of the many American students who studied tea and, yes, in an informal way, Zen with her—an accomplished spiritual master. She inspired affection and respect and was a second mother to many. In her quiet yet forceful and definite way, she expressed and embodied Zen spirit and continuity with the founder. She continued to live in the small apartment in the temple building, where she taught tea, cooked, cleaned, tended altars, and received guests. She was an anchor. As long as Okusan remained, as long as she went on day by day quietly expressing her life in engagement and sympathy with the community, things would be OK.

Suzuki Roshi died too soon. Even the most developed students he left behind were young and green, full of idealism and Zen theory and moxie but not enough maturity. They had not lived through the sorts of challenges that Okusan and her husband had experienced during their years in Japan and so had no basis for appreciating Zen as the religion it actually is—a powerful consolation and source of strength in times of suffering and instability. Okusan's presence expressed this strength and depth during the long years of Zen Center's rocky coming of age. She held down the fort, shored up the foundations. When that work was done, the maturity of the center established, she went home.

More than anything else, what Okusan taught in America was what Japan lacked after the war and perhaps still lacks—confidence in the depth of the Japanese way as formed by the culture's long encounter with the Buddhist teachings. Although she had studied tea casually as a child, it wasn't until she came to America that she began to study in earnest. Her practice of writing haiku also began in America, during the time when Suzuki Roshi first fell ill. How strange then that the powerful expression of her life, her essential Japaneseness—that elusive and almost ineffable feeling that unites tragedy, toughness, delicacy, beauty, and simplicity—was oddly never fully expressed in her until it came out in America, possibly as a way of coping with the strangeness, or maybe the pain, of living so many years among the people who had burned her country nearly to the ground—incomprehensible people, in many ways completely oblivious to who she was and what she had lived through—yet who, at the same time, perhaps understood and appreciated her more than anyone else ever had. Only in America did Mitsu Suzuki finally find and express her Japanese heart.

> I bow to my ballpoint pen
> and throw it out—
> year's end

....

Nothing could be more Japanese than haiku. As far as I know, nothing like it exists in any other language, though because of haiku's unique charm it has been exported into English and many other languages. It developed from *renga*, the linked verse form that was popular among the leisure classes in the earliest literate times in Japan. Renga was a sort of poetry parlor game. The first poet would write a provocative seventeen-syllable line. The next poet would cap the line with a second line of fourteen syllables, and a third would add another seventeen-syllable line, tying together as subtly and surprisingly as possible the implied intentions of the first two—and trying to surpass them. A fourth poet, with all this in mind, would add another line—and so on, long into the night, until a lengthy linked group poem had been produced, the more word play and literary and social jokes, the better. By the mid-fourteenth century, poets had begun writing terse, free-standing poems called *hokku*, which consisted only of the first seventeen-syllable renga line. This form later came to be called haiku and eventually developed a flavor independent of its origins. No longer social and sophisticated in tone, it became a unique form of religious or contemplative poetry. The essential Japanese aesthetic, inspired by Zen—emphasizing impermanence, the fleeting sadness and beauty of life, embeddedness in nature, a stoic sense of the humbleness of the human amid the vastness of the cosmos, simplicity, under- or unstated emotion—became the special province of haiku. By the seventeenth century, with Basho, haiku was fully developed as a form, with many variations.

In the early twentieth century, American poet Ezra Pound, among others, took up Chinese and Japanese poetry as an antidote to the conventional rhetoric that was smothering poetry in English. For Pound, Japanese poetry's emotional economy and, especially, its emphasis on the concrete image, was the answer. He called it imagism, and with it he revolutionized American poetry. Under Pound's influence, interest in haiku in America spread, with many poets, and other writers as disparate as Jack Kerouac and Richard Wright, taking up the form and making it self-consciously American. These days there are haiku clubs all over the United States, Japan, and many other places. Haiku has become, like renga, a group undertaking.

I mention all this because I believe that the poems in *A White Tea Bowl* come from and contribute to this hybrid international form we call haiku—which in turn comes from the spread and hybridization of Japanese culture and religion. Mitsu Suzuki's life embodies the Japanese spirit. Its circumstances dictated that she embrace and express that spirit so she could offer it to the American Zen students whom she lived among and nurtured for much of her adult life. But living in the United States, in the midst of the cultural ferment of the 1960s and beyond, in San Francisco, the epicenter of it all, how could she not also absorb its spirit? And how could that spirit not bleed into her writing? The quiet poems of *A White Tea Bowl*, like those of Mitsu's previous collection, *Temple Dusk*, express, in a subtle way impossible to define, the heart of a Zen life lived with loving integrity in turbulent times.

New Year's cards from friends—
colored patterns
of my life

....

Norman Fischer (Zoketsu) is a poet and author and a Zen Buddhist priest and teacher. His latest books are Training in Compassion *and* The Strugglers.

100 Haiku
from 100 Years of Life

TEMPLE BELLS

渓寺の鐘つき終わり新世紀

Tanidera no kane tsuki owari shinseiki

....

Valley temple bell—
with the last ring
a new century

方丈に「慈」の大軸や冬日射

Hōjō ni "ji" no ōjiku ya fuyu hizashi

....

In the abbot's quarters
"compassion" on a large scroll—
winter sunlight

提唱も坐禅も激し雷鳴裡

Teishō mo zazen mo hageshi raimei ri

....

Over and over
through dharma talk and zazen—
crashing thunder

釣り釜の小揺れ点前は若き僧

Tsuri gama no koyure temae wa wakaki sō

....

A young monk performs
tea ceremony—
hanging kettle sways slightly

方丈も見えて竹の子掘る日かな

Hōjō mo mie te takenoko horu hi kana

....

A day for digging
bamboo shoots—
even the abbot's here

ぼけよけの地蔵囲みし著莪の花

Bokeyoke no jizō kakomi shi shaga no hana

....

Jizō Bodhisattva
protector against dementia—
fringed iris

甘茶仏ただ法悦の大本堂

Amachabutsu tada hōetsu no daihondō

....

Great temple hall
I ladle sweet tea over Baby Buddha—
simple dharma bliss

新到の僧の面々風薫る

Shintō no sō no menmen kaze kaoru

....

Newly arrived monks
many faces—
fresh spring breeze

堂深く千手観音青葉冷ゆ

Dō fukaku senjukannon aoba hiyu

....

Deep in the temple
a thousand-armed Kannon—
coolness of green leaves

作務僧の一時みかんを囲みけり

Samu sō no ichiji mikan wo kakomi keri

....

Break from work practice
monks gather around—
mandarin oranges

梵鐘に夕茜して落ち葉焚く

Bonshō ni yū akane shi te ochiba taku

....

Temple bell
evening sky reddens—
burning autumn leaves

接心や坐堂に近く朴の花

Sesshin ya zadō ni chikaku hō no hana

....

During sesshin—
white magnolia blossoms
just outside the zendo

狛犬の大き口にも蝉時雨

Komainu no ōki kuchi ni mo semi shigure

....

Stone guardian dogs
mouths open wide—
torrent of cicada sound

鐘楼につかれぬ鐘や萩の露

Shōrō ni tsukare nu kane ya hagi no tsuyu

....

Old tower
bell hangs silent—
dew on bush clover

観音ののみ入れ式や竹の春

Kannon no nomiire shiki ya take no haru

....

Ceremony for carving
a statue of Kannon—
new bamboo leaves in autumn

突き終えし撞木の揺れや谷紅葉

Tsuki oe shi shumoku no yure ya tani momiji

....

When the temple bell is rung
the striker keeps swinging—
autumn colors in the valley

朝寒や暁坐にいそぐ僧の影

Asasamu ya gyōza ni isogu sō no kage

....

Cold dark morning—
monks' silhouettes
hurry to zazen

百八つ梵鐘の先平和あれ

Hyaku yattsu bonshō no saki heiwa are

....

The great temple bell rings
one hundred eight times—
May there be peace!

A WIDOW'S LIFE

初硯今日も初心と書きにけり

Hatsu suzuri kyō mo shoshin to kaki ni keri

....

First calligraphy of the year—
today again
I write "beginner's mind"

一輪のわびすけに笑む遺影かな

Ichirin no wabisuke ni emu iei kana

....

His portrait smiles—
a single
camellia blossom

春昼の一人に親し鳩時計

Haruhiru no hitori ni shitashi hatodokei

....

Spring midday—
in my solitude
the familiar cuckoo clock

桃の香と共に夢みし一夜かな

Momo no ka to tomo ni yume mi shi hitoya kana

....

Dreaming
all night long—
fragrance of peach blossoms

師の訃報語るともなく春しぐれ

Shi no fuhō kataru tomo naku haru shigure

....

No friend to share
news of my teacher's death—
spring rain

昼顔に思わず声をかけにけり

Hirugao ni omowa zu koe wo kake ni keri

....

Without thinking
I call out a greeting
to the "daytime-face" flower

何となく足の向く径ねぎ坊主

Nan to naku ashi no muku michi negi bōzu

....

Wandering where my feet lead me—
flowering scallions
like monks' shaven heads

庇陰の散歩に一句たまわ

Hisashi kage no sampo ni ikku tamawari nu

....

Walking in the shade of the eaves—
I receive
a single haiku

鈴虫と共に三日のお留守番

Suzumushi to tomo ni mikka no orusuban

....

Looking after the house—
alone for three days
with the bell crickets

お早うと木々に声かけ渓の径

Ohayō to kigi ni koe kake tani no michi

....

Good morning!
I greet one tree after another—
valley path

夏萩や世代の墓所へ径狭し

Natsuhagi ya sedai no bosho e michi semashi

....

Summer bush clover—
narrow path to the cemetery
graves of past abbots

一湾の凪ぎて港月止まりけり

Ichiwan no nagi te minatozuki tomari keri

....

The whole bay calm—
moon and harbor
still

晚秋の花火ふとみし己が影

Banshū no hanabi futo mi shi ono ga kage

....

Late autumn fireworks—
I suddenly glimpse
my own shadow

亡夫愛でし白磁茶碗に新茶汲む

Bōfu mede shi hakuji jawan ni shincha kumu

....

I pour shincha
into the white porcelain
tea bowl he loved

TELEくれる人もなくなり時雨空

Tele kureru hito mo naku nari shigurezora

···········

No one left
to give me a call—
drizzling autumn sky

古き文読み返しおり夜の秋

Furuki fumi yomi kaeshi ori yoru no aki

....

I read over
old letters—
autumn evening

方丈に遺影遺墨や実南天

Hōjō ni iei iboku ya minanten

....

In the abbot's quarters
his portrait and calligraphy—
red nanten berries

秋冷や茶碗のまろみ手に包む

Akibie ya chawan no maromi te ni tsutsumu

....

Autumn chill—
tea bowl's roundness
wrapped in my hands

庫裏に充つ風呂吹きの香や亡夫の忌

Kuri ni mitsu furofuki no ka ya bōfu no ki

....

In the temple kitchen
aroma of boiled daikon—
anniversary of his death

客去りて席中一人初時雨

Kyaku sari te sekichū hitori hatsushigure

....

Guests departed
alone in the tea room—
first winter rain

誰彼となく人恋し冬の夜

Dare kare to naku hito koishi fuyu no yoru

....

Winter night—
longing for company
anyone at all

大寒や剛直に伸ぶ枯芒

Daikan ya gōchokuni nobu kare susuki

....

Bitter cold—
dry pampas grass
stretches upright

散歩道日向日向を選びゆく

Sampo michi hinata hinata wo erabi yuku

....

Walking this path—
I choose one patch of sunlight
after another

THREE GENERATIONS

賀状みなわが人生の色模様

Gajō mina wa ga jinsei no iro moyō

....

New Year's cards from friends—
colored patterns
of my life

幼児とあそびゆっくり冬至風呂

Osanago to asobi yukkuri tōji buro

....

Leisurely bath
playing with the baby—
winter solstice

大寒や骨身惜しまぬ娘に合掌

Daikan ya honemi oshima nu ko ni gasshō

....

This bitter cold—
my daughter spares no effort
I bow in gratitude

沈丁花供華に句友の忌を修す

Jinchōge kuge ni kuyū no ki wo shūsu

....

I offer sweet daphne—
memorial service
for my haiku companion

三世代手つなぎ行くや梅祭り

San sedai te tsunagi yuku ya ume matsuri

....

Three generations
strolling hand in hand—
plum blossom festival

点滴の母を娘が押し野梅路を

Tenteki no haha wo ko ga oshi noume ji wo

....

Mother on intravenous
daughter pushing her wheelchair—
path of wild plums

新樹林みんな大地に還りゆく

Shinjurin minna daichi ni kaeri yuku

....

Fresh green woods—
everyone returns
to the great earth

笑い声先にかけられ春動く

Waraigoe saki ni kake rare haru ugoku

....

Her laughter
comes ahead to greet me —
spring in motion

「おめでとう」言いつつ散歩卒業日

"Omedetō" ii tsutsu sampo sotsugyōbi

....

"Congratulations!"
I say over and over
walking on graduation day

禅友を迎ふ参道法師蝉

Zen'yū wo mukau sandō hōshizemi

....

Greeting my Zen friend
coming up the temple path
"monk cicadas" chanting

すりこぎの三代古りしとろろ汁

Surikogi no sandai furi shi tororojiru

....

Mashing yams for soup
with this pestle
three generations old

日向ぼこ母の煙管の長かりし

Hinataboko haha no kiseru no nagaka ri shi

....

The long-stemmed pipe
my mother used to smoke
as she soaked up the sun

子の死をもわからぬ母に竹風鈴
Ko no shi wo mo wakara nu haha ni take fūrin

....

Bamboo wind chime—
she even forgets
her own child's death

桁台に祖母の名や秋彼岸

Kōdai ni sobo no na ya aki higan

....

My grandmother's name
on her kimono-hanging rack—
autumn equinox

大鍋のけんちん汁や娘も古希に

Ōnabe no kenchinjiru ya ko mo koki ni

....

Tofu vegetable soup—
a big pot for my daughter's
seventieth birthday

わだかまりほぐれし小春大小春

Wadakamari hogure shi koharu ōkoharu

....

Worries
come untangled—
little spring, great little spring

床上げの赤飯とどく秋日和

Tokoage no sekihan todoku akibyori

....

Well again after illness
a gift of red-bean rice—
clear autumn day

「飴おばさん」子等の寄り来て芽吹く園

"Ame Obasan" kora no yori ki te mebuku sono

....

"Candy Auntie!"
children run up to me—
buds swell in the garden

秋日和エアレター手に杖かろし

Akibiyori earetā te ni tsue karoshi

....

Clear autumn day—
airmail letter in my hand
walking stick feels light

黄楊櫛に残る母の香初時雨

Tsugegushi ni nokoru haha no ka hatsu shigure

....

Boxwood comb
my mother's fragrance—
first winter rain

小引き出整理の愉し年の暮

Kohikidashi seiri no tanoshi toshi no kure

....

Pleasure of organizing
small drawers—
year's end

献灯に逝きし子の名や村祭

Kentō ni yuki shi ko no na ya mura matsuri

....

Village festival—
votive lanterns with names
of children who have died

PEACH BLOSSOMS OPEN

歩道橋花吹雪中下校ベル

Hodōkyō hanafubuki chū gekō beru

············

Crossing the footbridge
blizzard of cherry petals—
end-of-day school bell

やさしさは命の雫里若葉

Yasashisa wa inochi no shizuku sato wakaba

....

Gentleness
life-giving raindrops—
village green leaves

桃咲きて柑樹のかげの薄れゆき

Momo saki te kanju no kage no usure yuki

....

Peach blossoms open—
the orange tree fades
into obscurity

梅雨明けて一湾の紺定まれり

Tsuyu ake te ichiwan no kon sadamare ri

....

End of rainy season—
the whole bay
smooth indigo

米搗きに鈴虫の音の高まれり

Kometsuki ni suzumushi no ne no takamare ri

....

Rising over the sound
of rice-cleaning—
bell crickets

白木蓮一瞬白の宇宙なり

Shiro mokuren isshun shiro no uchū nari

....

White magnolia blossoms—
for a moment
a white universe

殻ぬけし寡黙の蝉に朝の風

Kara nuke shi kamoku no semi ni asa no kaze

....

Shells cast off
cicadas silent—
morning breeze

コスモスに豆腐やラッパ流れゆく

Kosumosu ni tōfuya rappa nagare yuku

....

Cosmos flowers—
tofu vendor's horn
fades into the distance

ごみ置き場見守るごとく白芙蓉

Gomi okiba mimamoru gotoku shirofuyō

············

White rose-mallow
watching over the place
where we put out the garbage

厳然と見ゆる水門台風時

Genzen to miyuru suimon taifū ji

....

The flood gate
has a solemn look—
typhoon approaching

星とんで草原の夜の更けにけり

Hoshi ton de sōgen no yoru no fuke ni keri

....

A falling star
over the grassland—
night deepens

小夜時雨肩寄せ合ふて下る坂

Sayo shigure katayoseō te kudaru saka

....

Early autumn evening rain—
shoulders touching
they walk down the hill

八年目二つの柿が色づきぬ

Hachinemme futatsu no kaki iro zuki nu

....

At last two persimmons
ripen to deep orange—
eight-year-old tree

窯場まで銀杏落葉の道柔し

Kamaba made ichō ochiba no michi yawashi

....

Along the path to the kiln
golden gingko leaves
soft underfoot

墨色の雲の流れ八日月

Sumi iro no kumo no nagare yōka zuki

....

Ink-black clouds
stream past
waxing half-moon

深秋や山あじさいの錆色に

Shinshū ya yama ajisai no sabiiro ni

....

Deep autumn—
mountain hydrangeas
turned rust color

No Limit to Kindness

ふる里に根づきて拝む初の富士

Furusato ni nezuki te ogamu hatsu no Fuji

....

Rooted in my native place
I bow to Mount Fuji—
first view of the New Year

襟正し無事と書きけり初硯

Eri tadashi buji to kaki keri hatsu suzuri

....

Fastening my collar
I write "nothing special"—
first calligraphy of the year

やさしさに限りのなしや冬菫

Yasashisa ni kagiri no nashi ya fuyu sumire

....

No limit
to kindness—
winter violets

句にまなび句に支えられ露の道

Ku ni manabi ku ni sasae rare tsuyu no michi

....

Learning from haiku
sustained by haiku—
this path of dew

一つづゝ大事な仕事葉月ゆく

Hitotsu zutsu daijina shigoto hazuki yuku

....

Doing important tasks
one at a time—
month of green leaves passes

足袋つぎて八十路の一日足りにけり

Tabi tsugi te yasoji no ichinichi tari ni keri

....

I mend my tabi—
journey of my eightieth year
content with this day

句に暮れて句に明く日々や山笑う

Ku ni kure te ku ne aku hibi ya yama warau

....

Dusk falls with haiku
sun rises with haiku—
mountains smile

....

100 HAIKU FROM 100 YEARS OF LIFE | 111

年輪を九十六に風薫る

Nenrin wo kujūroku ni kaze kaoru

....

This tree of my life
has ninety-six rings—
fresh spring breeze

息止めているが如きに落椿

Iki tome te iru ga gotoki ni ochitsubaki

....

Like a breath
held—
fallen camellia

浄土への旅着をととのえ花筏

Jōdo e no tabigi totonoe hana ikada

....

I prepare clothing
for my journey to the Pure Land—
flower petals floating on water

耐へ耐へし暑さに今宵虫の声

Tae taeshi atsusa ni koyoi mushi no koe

....

Enduring the relentless heat
this evening—
insects singing

鈴虫を飼ひて命を思いけり

Suzumushi wo kai te inochi wo omoi keri

....

Feeding the bell crickets
I contemplate
life's brevity

杖の前バッタ飛び出す遠い富士

Tsue no mae batta tobidasu tōi Fuji

....

Grasshopper jumps out
in front of my walking stick—
distant Fuji

言の葉を見出し得ずや落葉踏む

Koto no ha wo miidashi e zu ya ochiba fumu

....

Leaves of speech—
unable to put words in order
I stamp through fallen leaves

一物も持たぬ生死や秋うらら

Ichimotsu mo mota nu shōji ya aki urara

....

Birth and death
not holding on to even one thing—
autumn brightness

年輪を重ねしお灰風炉点前

Nenrin wo kasane shi ohai furo temae

....

On many years' ash—
I light the charcoal
for tea ceremony

無事習ふ日々の暮らしや秋深む

Buji narau hibi no kurashi ya aki fukamu

....

Learning to be "nothing special"
day by day—
autumn deepens

利他行と心にしかと寒の朝

Ritagyō to kokoro ni shika to kan no asa

....

To be of benefit to others
my heart's firm vow—
cold winter morning

冬かさね手足に感謝ゆめ愉し

Fuyu kasane teashi ni kansha yume tanoshi

....

Winter after winter
grateful for hands and feet—
life a pleasant dream

ボールペン合掌裡に捨つ年の暮れ

Bōrupen gasshōri ni sute tsu toshi no kure

....

I bow to my ballpoint pen
and throw it out—
year's end

PICKLES AND TEA:

Remembrances of Mitsu Suzuki

Reb Anderson

When Suzuki Roshi was alive, Okusan would often invite Zen students to her kitchen for tea with Suzuki Roshi and herself. She served the tea with a variety of pickled vegetables that she made herself. After Suzuki Roshi died, she continued the practice of inviting us to tea. During these teas, she would sometimes talk to me about rather serious matters related to our life and practice. On one of these occasions, in reference to things going on at Zen Center, she said, "When we take care of something for a long time we may come to think that we own it."

In the mid-eighties, in the midst of the turmoil around spiritual leadership, our students were so upset and frustrated that they became angry and sometimes overlooked our practice of respecting others and studying the self. Okusan, seeing this, said to me, "Suzuki Roshi's way is not to hate people."

Virginia Baker once asked Okusan what the most important thing to teach kindergartners was. Okusan said, "*Gassho.*" (To gassho is to join the palms of the hands together and bow in a formal greeting.)

One day, cookies were being served on a tray and she was asked, "Which one should I take?"

"The one nearest to you," she replied.

I formally addressed Okusan as Shibo, which is translated from Chinese literally as "teacher mother." I always remember with gratitude her nourishing teachings.

....

Reb Anderson (Tenshin Zenki) is Senior Dharma Teacher and former abbot of San Francisco Zen Center. He is the author of Warm Smiles from Cold Mountains, Being Upright, *and* The Third Turning of the Wheel.

PAUL ROSENBLUM

In 1983, after Baker Roshi left San Francisco Zen Center, many students in the City Center on Page Street seemed to be disillusioned, disappointed, disgruntled, and even despairing. Participation in the daily schedule had fallen off significantly. There were a lot of empty seats in the zendo and the Buddha Hall. Okusan on more than one occasion commented, "Just one person. If just one person comes, that is enough."

Many of us felt her kind, selfless regard, always looking out for us and our well-being, in accord with Suzuki Roshi's wish: that she remain after he died and help Zen Center. It might have been easier for her to return to Japan, but her priority was to fulfill his request and to support our practice. She did this wholeheartedly, generously, and unselfishly for more than twenty years. She embodied a spirit and way of being that continues to inform and encourage me.

I have a blood disorder, a form of hemophilia, so my doctors advise me to regularly eat meat. In spite of our vegetarian diet, Okusan made an effort to bring me meat. Often, after she returned from a special meal out, I would find a small package of food she claimed was "left over" from her meal. I frequently had the feeling that she left a part of her meal unfinished so she would have something for me. I really enjoyed these treats and appreciated how she continually was looking after me, caring for my well-being.

Okusan has a rare mix of directness, fairness, and honesty, and at the same time she is lighthearted and playful. She does not mince words. Once, when my mother came from New York to visit me, I invited Okusan to meet her. Upon being introduced, Okusan announced, "You know, I am his Japanese mother!" We invited her to join us for dinner and went to a French restaurant with very dim lights. The waiter gave Okusan and my mother small pink flashlights to help them read the menu. They both immediately began playing with the flashlights, switching them on and off, shining them not only on the menu but also on each other, me, the walls, the ceiling—everywhere. They got along splendidly.

I would often buy fresh flowers for the Kaisando—the Founder's Hall dedicated to Suzuki Roshi—delivering them to Okusan on Fridays after returning from work downtown. She began in an informal way to teach me about flowers, showing me how to arrange them first in the hand, then cutting them and placing them in a vase. She chose vases with a neck and did not use those requiring a *kenzan*— the needlepoint holder—that is often associated with traditional flower arranging. She said she did this so as to not hurt the flowers.

I have fond memories of intimate moments, sitting in her kitchen, talking together while drinking green tea from light blue teacups with dark blue rims and munching on her wonderful homemade pickles (the turnip ones were a particular favorite). She would say, "Paul-san, I made some pickles. Would you like some?"

....

Paul Rosenblum (Ryuten) began Zen practice with Shunryu Suzuki Roshi at Tassajara in 1968. He is a disciple and a successor of Zentatsu Baker Roshi and currently practices and teaches at Johanneshof / Genrin-ji in the Black Forest, Germany, as well as with groups in Europe and the United States.

PETER COYOTE

I arrived at San Francisco Zen Center in 1974. The great master, Shunryu Suzuki, had already died, and I was saddened by my bad luck in having missed meeting this inspirational man, from whose vision three vibrant Zen Centers—San Francisco City Center, Green Gulch Farm, and Tassajara Zen Mountain Center—were even then functioning and teaching the dharma.

Marilyn McCann, the girl I lived with, who subsequently became my wife, was a student of formal Japanese tea ceremony, and her teacher was the widow of Suzuki Roshi, Mitsu Suzuki. Marilyn was already an advanced Zen student and had such unqualified respect for her teacher that it whetted my curiosity about her.

I observed Mrs. Suzuki carefully whenever I saw her, hoping to learn some clues about her husband and what I imagined to be "secrets of Zen" he might have imparted to her. She was a tiny person, perhaps under five feet tall, usually dressed in either tea ceremony kimonos or the ubiquitous "fat-pants" and *hippari* (a jacket fastened by ties) of Zen practitioners. She was extremely quiet, and appeared to take up no space in the room. Her face was often cast in a grave and dignified expression, and she transmitted the impression of a discriminating but not judgmental watchfulness. Occasionally I saw signs of a merry twinkle in her expression, which suggested that there might be deeper water under her placid surface.

Because my wife studied with her every week (and continued for over twenty years, eventually becoming a fully accredited Omote Senke tea teacher), I had ample opportunity to observe Okusan (Japanese for "Mother," how she was normally addressed). We lived directly across the street, and it was easy to encounter her in the neighborhood grocery store or walking through the halls of Zen Center.

One day I informed her that I was an actor. Her eyes lit up, and she cocked her head and pantomimed looking up at me from far below. "Ahhhh, great actor," she said with a joyful smile. "Toshiro Coyote," she added and giggled like a schoolgirl. I was bowled over, and because her English was a bit spotty and my Japanese nonexistent, I immediately imitated Toshiro Mifune in one of his scowling samurai roles, hand on the hilt of an invisible sword. She laughed and clapped her hands delightedly at my foolishness.

I soon learned that her two modes, a rather daunting formalism and a wicked sense of play and fun, are common in Japanese culture. If she were a sea, there would be playful whitecaps cavorting on depths of truly deep water. Her mirth was absolutely sincere, but it never erased the existence of a highly observant consciousness below it.

One night, after my wife and I had moved to the suburbs, we invited Okusan to dinner at our house in Mill Valley. At some point during the dinner, Okusan looked at me and said, "Peter-san, you look cold." I thanked her for her concern but assured her that I was just fine, completely comfortable, and I continued eating, marveling at how considerate she was. Ten minutes later, she rose and returned to the table, wrapping a shawl about her shoulders. I felt like a fool. From her perspective it would have appeared self-concerned to say, "I am cold." It might have made me feel inadequate or thoughtless as a host. Her indirection had afforded me the opportunity to resolve the situation with no suggestion of error on my part, had I been alert enough.

I think that was the first time I actually apprehended the subtlety of Okusan, and I resolved to know her better and to learn from her. I could never know her husband, but they had lived together a long time, and I assumed that, in the manner in which couples often achieve a metamorphosis of one into another, her years of intimate exposure to Zen might be available to me if I searched deeply enough. I was, by that time, a serious Zen student with an awakened curiosity about the practice.

I began taking the occasional tea with her in the afternoons—informally, in her kitchen. She lived in a tiny apartment with none of the self-conscious "Zen" feeling of the rest of the temple. She kept food in Tupperware containers and made tea informally in simple cups and a pot. She fed me *hijiki* and *kimpira* and appeared to be delighted that I appreciated them. I sometimes took her on outings in San Francisco, and she introduced me to a side of Japantown heretofore invisible to me, where the deep bows and respect tendered to her demonstrated how high her status was in the world outside our cloistered community.

One day, during tea, she passed me a plate of little jelly-like tea sweets. They were cut in uneven sizes, and when she offered the plate to me, I paused to review before choosing, not wanting to take the biggest piece and appear greedy. She caught my deliberation instantly and said, "Always closest! Sometimes biggest, sometimes smallest." I was astonished enough that she had observed my wavering, but more astonished that she had worked out a simple rule for herself for such an insignificant incident, a rule that made it possible for her to act instinctively, without confusion.

Okusan's simplicity, directness, and honesty became a guidepost and beacon for me that has remained as bright thirty-nine years later as it was the first day I met her.

....

Peter Coyote came from nowhere and is working his way back! An ordained Zen priest in the lineage of Shunryu Suzuki Roshi. Father of two. Addicted to old vehicles.

VICTORIA AUSTIN

When I entered the room for my first lesson in tea ceremony from Suzuki Sensei, my first impression was of immaculate spring light and a sweet smell. Water was bubbling in a large iron pot, and steam mingled with fragrant incense. Under a scroll was a polished piece of wood on which a single flower in a vase stood. The floor was four-and-one-half tatami mats (each mat is about three by six feet), so clean that they seemed to glow. Next to the door was a set of plain wood shelves with mysterious bowls, ladles, and bamboo utensils whose colors seemed unusually vivid for such subdued, natural shades. All those impressions registered in my stomach in an instant.

Before I had a chance to think, Suzuki Sensei said, "Please wash your hands with soap and dry them on the towel next to the sink." Then she taught me how to say "good morning" and ask for her teaching in Japanese: "*Ohayo gozaimasu, Sensei. Onegai itashimasu.*" She brought out a thermos, a bowl, and a tray, and taught me how to receive a teacake and how to eat and drink. She assigned me a partner, another student who looked as awkward as I felt. We practiced saying the unfamiliar words.

Over the next few sessions I realized that teaching tea wasn't easy for her. Just as in sewing class, here too our instincts were all backwards from her teaching. Despite my intention to change my habit, day after day I would impolitely reach for tea objects with my left hand. From *seiza*, Suzuki Sensei would tap my hands with a ladle handle or a fan: "Vicki-san! Every time the same mistake! Why do you want to study tea?"

Another time, as I was scooping some powdered tea into the tea bowl, I accidentally dropped a small amount onto the tatami mat. She silently brought a damp cloth, then wiped up the mess, while I sat there feeling like an idiot. I had ruined the whole occasion. I didn't know what to say. She said, "Please apologize," and I did.

Once someone dropped the tea bowl and it broke. Half-laughing, Suzuki Sensei said, "In Japan you would have to commit suicide if you did something like this." Many years later, she fleetingly considered teaching us *kaiseki*, the formal meal service that precedes the tea ceremony. "No," she decided. "I don't want to go crazy, and I don't want you to go crazy."

Prodding ladles, persistent left-handedness, my awkwardness, and the knee pain from sitting so long—sometimes I would get so frustrated and impatient, and in my discouragement I would think, "This is too hard, too foreign. It's obvious I'll never get it. I should just quit right now." Again and again I watched Suzuki Sensei pick up the bowl, the fan, and the ladle in the proper way, with presence and dignity. As I practiced her corrections and imitated her example, eventually I realized that the difficulty had become a challenge and the foreignness, a broader perspective. But my mental and physical attitudes took a long time to change. Only now am I beginning to see the kind of patience that allowed her to sit next to me and correct me all those times.

When Suzuki Sensei saw large, clumsy America students like me enter the tearoom, she wasn't repulsed or disturbed. She didn't reject us or grab onto us. Instead, she simply showed us the next step of the tea ceremony. She taught our feet to touch the floor when they walk and our hands to feel the warmth of the bowl changing as we held it in our hands.

....

Victoria Austin (Shosan) started sitting zazen in 1971, received dharma transmission in Shunryu Suzuki Roshi's lineage from Sojun Mel Weitsman in 1999, and currently teaches at San Francisco Zen Center. She studied sewing, tea, and human life with Mitsu Suzuki Sensei from 1975 to 1993.

YVONNE RAND

In the 1960s I became the secretary for the San Francisco Zen Center. At that time Zen Center was still located on Bush Street, in the temple for the Japanese community in and around San Francisco, called Soko-ji. The Japanese community in San Francisco had invited Suzuki Roshi to be the priest at Soko-ji. He arrived in the United States first, and Okusan followed later. Once she arrived, she took her place as a clear-minded wife who stood in her own shoes and asserted herself vigorously and authoritatively, to a degree unusual for a woman in Japanese culture. To my eyes, she enjoyed the authority she commanded, and it played a large part in the way she approached and managed her marriage and her life.

Okusan knew how to take care of Suzuki Roshi as well as other members of the Zen community. She took care by supporting people, Suzuki Roshi in particular, and attending to their needs. And she also took care of people, Suzuki Roshi in particular, by making sure that the conduct of both the Japanese and the Americans who came under her sway was appropriate, as she determined appropriateness. She was equally demanding of herself.

My desk was in a room on the first floor of the Bush Street temple. I shared the space with Katagiri Roshi. At that time, he was still Katagiri Sensei. Katagiri was the father of two young children, and he was often up with the children during the night and was frequently exhausted in the morning. Nevertheless he was punctually present each day for early morning zazen practice, but at some cost to his energy. Often Katagiri Sensei would seek some rest by napping on the sofa in our office.

Napping was not acceptable conduct under Okusan's regime. She knew that Katagiri was a secret napper, and she would endeavor to catch him transgressing. But when she descended the stairs from the Suzuki quarters upstairs to our first-floor office, her slippers produced an audible slap-slap-slap on the stair treads as she made her way down. The sound provided enough of a warning for me to be able to whisper to Katagiri to get up in time to be seated at his desk, seemingly alert and busy, before Okusan entered for her inspection. I remember her as being quite fierce. I think she suspected what we were up to but was never able to prove it and call Katagiri and me to account for our conspiratorial disobedience.

Once I drove Suzuki Roshi and Okusan from Tassajara to San Francisco. We stopped for lunch at a restaurant in Monterey. Our table was near the windows, through which we could overlook the Pacific Ocean beyond the city of Monterey. I remember Okusan being rather stern with Suzuki Roshi for looking out the window instead of attending to his lunch.

Okusan's steadiness and devotion to Suzuki Roshi was apparent during his final illness and as he was dying at San Francisco Zen Center. I sat with him at night, and Okusan took the day shift, caring for him all day as his life was ending. The day before he died, he took a bath as part of readying himself for passing over. He took his last breath just after the bell began ringing to announce the start of the Winter Retreat.

....

Yvonne Rand (JiKai Myo-on) is a meditation teacher and lay householder priest in the Soto Zen Buddhist tradition. She began her practice and study of Zen with Shunryu Suzuki Roshi in 1966. She incorporates insights from the psychotherapy traditions in her teaching and investigates the relevance of the arts and gardening for training the mind.

MARY WATSON

I had the great honor of studying Japanese tea ceremony with Okusan for sixteen years, from 1977 until 1993 when she moved back to Japan to live with her daughter.

I've never forgotten my very first tea ceremony. Okusan had told us to bring pencils, and I forgot mine. Although she did not say anything, I certainly had a pencil with me for tea lessons from then on. From that very first day, when Sensei showed us how to hold and turn a tea bowl correctly, I realized that learning tea ceremony was going to be exacting and a real challenge.

The practice of tea has always been for me a concentrated practice in mindfulness and learning to make mistakes with grace. I remember once in Okusan's small tearoom, I was walking toward the teakettle, holding a tea bowl and the container of powdered tea. My mind drifted, Okusan simply cleared her throat, and I was back, just walking toward the teakettle. I've always wondered how she was able to know my mind.

On a spring morning in 1992, I came across Okusan in the Zen Center courtyard, looking at a morning glory. Just by noticing how she looked at the flower, I saw the miracle of how the bud unfurled.

In the early days, before our lesson, she would make an offering to Suzuki Roshi, whose picture was on her bureau in the tearoom. Sometimes she would just talk to him, saying that she hoped he would enjoy the tea she had made for him.

Often we would hold special gatherings, some just for her students and others for the larger Omote Senke tea community, for New Year or to honor certain tea masters. We would have tea together and then go out to a Japanese restaurant. At the end of the meal, Okusan would sing songs she used to sing to her kindergarten class in Japan. She sang wonderfully, with great enthusiasm and vigor. I understand that now, at nearly one hundred years of age, she is still singing!

....

Mary Watson (Gen Ji Iku Shi) has been an active member of Zen Center since the 1970s. She studied tea with Suzuki Sensei for sixteen years and considers it one of the most important things she has done in her life.

Edward Espe Brown

In many ways Suzuki Sensei was the mother that I never had, giving me a model or template for how to mother myself and others. Once when I was the *tenzo* (head cook) at Tassajara in the 1960s, Okusan came to visit and gave me a present of a box of mixed salted nuts. It seemed like such a blessing as well as a confirmation of my practice and my standing in the community. Immediately upon receiving them I thought, "Oh, I will certainly share these with others." After the box sat unopened for days, I finally opened it and ate one. That nut was so delicious: salty, oily, nutty, crunchy. Heavenly! Eating just a few each day, I managed to make the box last for two weeks or more, savoring Okusan's kindness in each bite, nut by nut, along with my shame for not sharing them.

In September 1971 I was ordained as Suzuki Roshi's disciple in a ceremony at the City Center. Without telling me why, Roshi had delayed my ordination, thinking that I was more interested in starting a bakery. Finally, during a tea class, Okusan passed on this information to my wife, Meg, who responded, "Oh no, that's not right. Ed wants to be a priest." Soon after, I had *dokusan*, a formal meeting with

Roshi, who said, "If you become a priest, you cannot be a baker. Is that clear?" I agreed, absolutely. Thanks to Oku-san's ability to finesse it, I was ordained as Roshi's disciple.

In the mid-1970s, after Suzuki Roshi had died, we were living at the City Center. Whenever I was sick, a ceramic cup of *chawan mushi* set on a small wooden dish would show up on the concrete floor just outside my door. The Japanese egg custard would have a few pieces of vegetable and often a small piece of chicken or shrimp, along with a ceramic lid on top. Chawan mushi never tasted so good. And I would know that Suzuki Sensei cared deeply for me. She was noticing me and tending to my welfare.

I lived at the City Center for five years and then across the street in an apartment for five years, from 1974 to 1983. They were dark, difficult years, as I was getting divorced and was no longer in alignment with Suzuki Roshi's successor, Baker Roshi. Whenever things hit the lowest of the low, Suzuki Sensei would notice: "Edo-san, would you like some tea?" And I would come to her door at the end of the hall and be invited into her little kitchen. "Please, have a seat."

I felt so received, so taken in, so honored to be in her space. I would watch as she heated water, poured it in the Elephant thermos and into the teapot to preheat it, then emptied the water. "Edo-san, you love pickles, yes?" I watched as she put green tea in the pot, filled the cups with hot water, then let the water cool slightly before pouring it into the teapot. "Edo-san, you like your tea strong, don't you?"

We would eat pickles and sip tea, not solving or fixing anything. When I was particularly discouraged or depressed, she would say mischievously, "Edo-san, would you like a glass of wine?"

"No, thank you," I would reply. Being in her company was carrying me along.

"Toast?"

"No, thank you. I'm fine, just fine."

And always to myself I would be saying, "Okusan, thank you. I'll be okay. I have a place at your table. That means the world to me."

....

Edward Espe Brown was ordained as a disciple of Shunryu Suzuki Roshi on September 11, 1971, and given the name Jusan Kainei, Longevity Mountain Peaceful Sea. He is the editor of a book of Roshi's talks called Not Always So.

Afterword

Kate McCandless

The inspiration for this book project came from my 2010 meeting with Suzuki Sensei described by Norman Fischer in his introduction. I had not known Sensei in her years at San Francisco Zen Center, but I was deeply moved by the grace and vitality of her presence at such an advanced age. It seemed her life had something more to teach those who continue to remember and benefit from her husband's teachings—and what better way to share those teachings than through her haiku.

In May 2013, I again had the good fortune to spend several days at Rinso-in with a group of sangha members from Mountain Rain Zen Community. Suzuki Sensei had been quite ill a month before, but she had rallied, and was well enough for me to visit, along with her granddaughter-in-law, Kumi-san. She was clearly frailer than she had been three years earlier.

When I showed her a draft of the translation, she told me that Suzuki Roshi had left her two gifts before he died. One was the advice to slow down and take life at a more leisurely pace—she'd been known for bustling about Zen Center, taking care of everything. The second gift was his suggestion that she take up writing haiku. Perhaps he had intuited both her ability and her need to express herself.

Looking over the manuscript, she and her daughter reminisced. "Oh, that persimmon tree! It snapped off in a big storm. But now it's sending up new shoots from the root." Sensei remembered the long walks she used to take along the banks of a small river, with a view of Mt. Fuji in the distance. "Getting old is hard," she said, as she moved to a chair from the tatami. But as I said good-bye, her eyes were bright and her hands firmly held mine. "Good girl, I'm proud of you," she said, to my surprise. Then she switched back to Japanese: "They were the first English words I learned from Wilkinson Sensei." He was the Canadian Christian missionary who taught her so many years ago.

The mind reels to think of all that has happened in this world in the hundred years this one small, dauntless woman has lived and how her life has been shaped by great forces of change. But the gift of her haiku is simple and ordinary. The Japanese say, *ichigo ichie,* one meeting, one moment.

Thank you, Sensei, for meeting us—and happy birthday!

Editor's Acknowledgments

Kazuaki Tanahashi

Every human life is a miracle. A life of one hundred years is a miracle of miracles. This book is born of joy and best wishes by some of the many who love and adore Mitsu Suzuki.

I had the pleasure of meeting her and her husband, Zen master Shunryu Suzuki, when I made a brief visit to Soko-ji Temple in San Francisco in January 1964. She had moved from Japan a few years before to assist her husband, who was serving as priest for the Japanese American members of the temple and also teaching Zen to non-Japanese practitioners. Mitsu told me a story of her experience of arriving in this new country, not knowing how to get off the city bus, and being helped by other passengers. I did not know at that time that she was nearly fifty years old. That makes it that I have known her slightly more than half of her life.

After making one more visit to Soko-ji in 1965, I went back to Japan. Twelve years later, when I returned to the city to work for the San Francisco Zen Center as a scholar-in-residence, the widowed Mitsu Suzuki remained living in the former-abbot's quarters, on the second floor of the large brick building of the Zen Center. She was teaching tea ceremony and keeping the practicing Zen community warm and homey, as her husband had wished her to do. Mitsu and I ran into each other in the building and on the street. She would invite me to tea gatherings with her Japanese teacher and peers. I was her translator when she gave brief speeches. With one of her tea students, Gregory Wood, I translated her haiku into English and got it published before her seventieth birthday. *Temple Dusk* has now been translated into German and Hebrew.

In 2010, Kate McCandless, a Zen teacher at Mountain Rain Zen Community in Vancouver, Canada, told me that she wanted to translate Mitsu Suzuki's recent haiku. I thought it was a wonderful idea. So in September 2012, with my daughter Karuna, I visited Mitsu and asked her if she would let us copy her poems. She lent us six notebooks that contained four thousand haiku she had written after returning to Japan. Karuna and I copied them in Kyoto. Some of the haiku had marks indicating that she had submitted them to some haiku magazines. She also had been a regular contributor to *Sansho*, the magazine of Eihei-ji temple, which has a section of members' haiku. Following Mitsu's notations and using my own judgment, I selected and typed about 140 haiku for Kate.

My deep appreciations go to Kate for her initial wish and her tremendous effort studying and translating the haiku for *A White Tea Bowl*. My gratitude goes to Norman

Fischer for his illuminating introduction. Thanks to David Chadwick for providing accurate information on the life of Mitsu through his research for his acclaimed biography of Shunryu Suzuki, *Crooked Cucumber*. We are fortunate to have firsthand reflections of Mitsu by Reb Anderson, Victoria Austin, Ed Brown, Peter Coyote, Yvonne Rand, Paul Rosenblum, and Mary Watson. Thanks to Roberta Werdinger for her initial editing of these accounts and to Nigel Black for his draft cover design. Thanks to Karuna Tanahashi, Linda Hess, and Susan O'Leary for their help. Thanks to Mitsue Nagase for her photography. My gratitude to Victoria Shoemaker for representing me and to the San Francisco Zen Center for holding the copyright on behalf of the author.

Thanks to Donald Moyer and Holly Hammond for editing, and to Gopa and Veetam Campbell at Gopa & Ted2, Inc. for design.

TRANSLATOR'S ACKNOWLEDGEMENTS
Kate McCandless

First, my deep gratitude to Kazuaki Tanahashi for trusting me to undertake this translation and for his wisdom, knowledge, and support along the way. Warm thanks also to Peter Levitt for his perceptive reading and for asking the right questions, to Michael Newton for faithful and observant reading and rereading, to Takeo Yamashiro and Kazuko Ikegawa for their native-speakers' perspectives, and of course, deep bows to Suzuki Sensei for her shining practice and example.

This translation is dedicated to my mother, Margaret McCandless, who is ninety years old and has shared many haiku moments with me.

Notes

17   *last ring*: On New Year's Eve at midnight, all over Japan, Buddhist temple bells are rung 108 times, to dispel each of our 108 delusions. People walk to their local temple and line up in hopes of getting to ring the bell. These large bells hang in an outdoor bell tower; they have no clapper and are rung by being struck by a log striker suspended from ropes.

19   *dharma talk (teishō)*: a formal talk given by a Zen teacher

      zazen: sitting meditation

22   *bodhisattva (awakening being)*: a being who vows not to attain complete enlightenment until all beings are enlightened. Different archetypal bodhisattvas in Buddhist literature and iconography have particular attributes through which they alleviate suffering.

      Jizō (Sanskrit: *Kshitigarbha*): Depicted as a shaven-headed monk, he is the bodhisattva known for his great vow to continue the Buddha's work of saving all beings from suffering. In Japan he is beloved as the protector of women, children, and travelers. At the entrance to the Rinsō-in cemetery is a large stone Jizō image. At his feet, instead of the usual image of babies or small children, are an old man and woman in childlike form. This Jizō is called the dementia-preventing Jizō.

23   *I ladle sweet tea over Baby Buddha*: Buddha's birthday, in Japan called Hanamatsuri (Flower Festival), is celebrated on

April 8. At Buddhist temples a small pavilion decorated with flowers is set up, sheltering an image of the Buddha as a baby. Worshippers "bathe" the baby Buddha by ladling sweet green tea over the image.

24 *newly arrived monks*: A new cohort of novice monks typically arrives each spring at Eiheiji, the monastery deep in the mountains of western Japan, where Shunryu Suzuki, his son, and his grandson each trained.

25 *Kannon* (Sanskrit: *Avalokiteshvara*): the bodhisattva of compassion, in Japan often depicted in female form. One variation is the thousand-armed Kannon, who holds a different tool in each hand for relieving the many kinds of human suffering.

28 *sesshin*: a period of intensive Zen meditation practice, usually lasting five to seven days

    zendo: a hall for Zen practice

31 *Kannon*: See above.

37 *beginner's mind*: a Zen phrase, referring to a mind with the capacity to meet each moment with openness and flexibility. It has become well-known in the West through its use in the title of the classic *Zen Mind, Beginner's Mind*, by Shunryu Suzuki. As he says: "In the beginner's mind there are many possibilities; in the expert's mind there are few."

38 *his portrait*: a formal memorial portrait photo, displayed at a funeral, and often kept on the family altar thereafter

42 *"daytime-face" flower (hirugao)*: *Calystegia japonica*, a bindweed. The morning glory is called the "morning-face" (*asagao*), and the moonflower is called the "evening-face" (*yūgao*).

45 *bell crickets (suzumushi)*: *Homeogryllus japonicas*, crickets with a bell-like call, traditionally kept in cages and fed so that their song can be enjoyed

47 *past abbots*: Rinsō-in, the temple Suzuki Roshi left when he went to San Francisco, and of which his son Hōitsu Suzuki is abbot today, sits at the foot of High Grass Mountain beneath a bamboo grove. Behind the temple, up a steep narrow path, is a small cemetery where the ashes of many generations of former abbots are interred.

50 *shincha*: green tea made from the first picking of tea leaves each year

51 *TELE*: Japanese is a flexible language that can include alphabetic letters or words in their sentences, sometimes in abbreviation. In this case, "telephone" is abbreviated as "tele."

53 *his portrait and calligraphy*: memorial portrait and calligraphy often displayed on an altar

55 *anniversary of his death*: Shunryu Suzuki Roshi died on December 3, 1971, at San Francisco Zen Center.

71 *graduation day*: The Japanese school year begins in April and ends when graduation takes place the following February or March.

72 *"monk cicadas" (hōshizemi)*: *Meimuna opalifera*, a kind of cicada with a loud, monotonous song, also called *tsukutsuku-boshi* in Japanese.

73 *yams for soup (tororojiru)*: *tororo*, a white yam, which when grated makes a mucilaginous soup, often served chilled

74 *long-stemmed pipe*: smoked by both men and women in pre-modern Japan

78 *little spring*: the Japanese expression for Indian summer, a warm, sunny period in autumn

79 *red-bean rice (sekihan)*: rice cooked with azuki beans, eaten on celebratory occasions

82 *boxwood comb*: Boxwood was traditionally used for carved hair ornaments and combs because of its pleasant fragrance.

106 *"nothing special"* (*buji*): A Zen expression, literally "no thing," refers to nonattachment.

110 *tabi*: white cotton socks with a separate big toe, worn with traditional Japanese footwear

114 *Pure Land* (*jōdo*): the realm of Amida Buddha, where he receives believers who have died and leads them to enlightenment

116 *bell crickets*: See above. Bell crickets are short-lived.

118 *leaves of speech* (*kotoba*): The word for "words" or "language" in Japanese is *kotoba*, literally "speech leaves."

121 *"nothing special"*: See above.

ABOUT THE AUTHOR

 Mitsu was born to the Sakai family in Shizuoka City, Japan, on April 23, 1914. After losing her first husband in the Sino-Japanese War, she graduated from the Nara Advanced Woman Teachers School. In 1950 she became the principal of the Tokiwa Kindergarten, affiliated with Rinso-in Zen Temple, Yaizu City, Shizuoka Prefecture. She married Shunryu Suzuki, abbot of the temple, in 1958. Shunryu left for San Francisco to be the abbot of Soko-ji Temple in 1959, and Mitsu joined him in 1961. Shunryu and his community moved to the current San Francisco Zen Center location in 1969. After founding the Zen Center's Zen Mountain Center at Tassajara in 1971, he passed away in December of the same year. Mitsu stayed at San Francisco Zen Center until 1993. She now resides in Shizuoka City. Her book of haiku *Temple Dusk* was published by Parallax Press in 1992.

About the Editor

Kazuaki Tanahashi is an artist, Buddhist scholar, writer, translator, and peace worker. His numerous books include *Enlightenment Unfolds, Brush Mind,* and *Sky Above, Great Wind.* Born in Japan in 1933, he first came to the United States in 1977, and now lives in Berkeley, California.

About the Translator

Kate McCandless is a poet, translator, and Soto Zen priest in the lineage of Shunryu Suzuki Roshi. She is a resident teacher at Mountain Rain Zen Community in Vancouver, British Columbia.

FROM THE PUBLISHER

Shambhala Publications is pleased to publish the Rodmell Press collection of books on yoga, Buddhism, and aikido. As was the aspiration of the founders of Rodmell Press, it is our hope that these books will help individuals develop a more skillful practice—one that brings peace to their daily lives and to the Earth.

To learn more, please visit www.shambhala.com.